STAR WARS™

WORKBOOKS

NUMBER FUN

FOR AGES 4–5

BY THE EDITORS OF BRAIN QUEST

■SCHOLASTIC

Scholastic Children's Books
Euston House,
24 Eversholt Street,
London NW1 1DB, UK

A division of Scholastic Ltd
London ~ New York ~ Toronto ~ Sydney ~ Auckland
Mexico City ~ New Delhi ~ Hong Kong

First published in the USA by Workman Publishing in 2014.
This edition published in the UK by Scholastic Ltd in 2015.

© & TM 2015 LUCASFILM LTD.

STAR WARS is a registered trademark of Lucasfilm Ltd.
BRAIN QUEST is a registered trademark of Workman Publishing Co., Inc., and Groupe Play Bac, S.A.

Workbook series design by Raquel Jaramillo
Cover illustration by Mike Sutfin
Interior illustrations by Pat Pigott and Mike Gorman

ISBN 978 1407 16281 2

Printed in the UK by Bell and Bain Ltd, Glasgow

6 8 10 9 7 5

Papers used by Scholastic Children's Books are made from woods grown in sustainable forests.

www.scholastic.co.uk

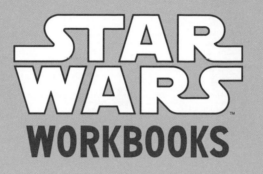

STAR WARS™

WORKBOOKS

This workbook belongs to:

_____

0 zero

This is zero, the number 0.

0 stands for none.

Trace each 0.

Start at the red dot.

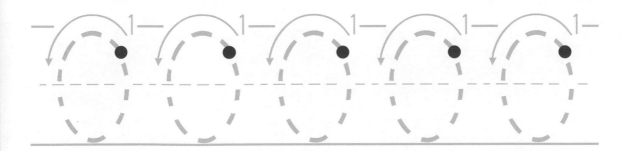

Circle the galaxies that have **0** planets.

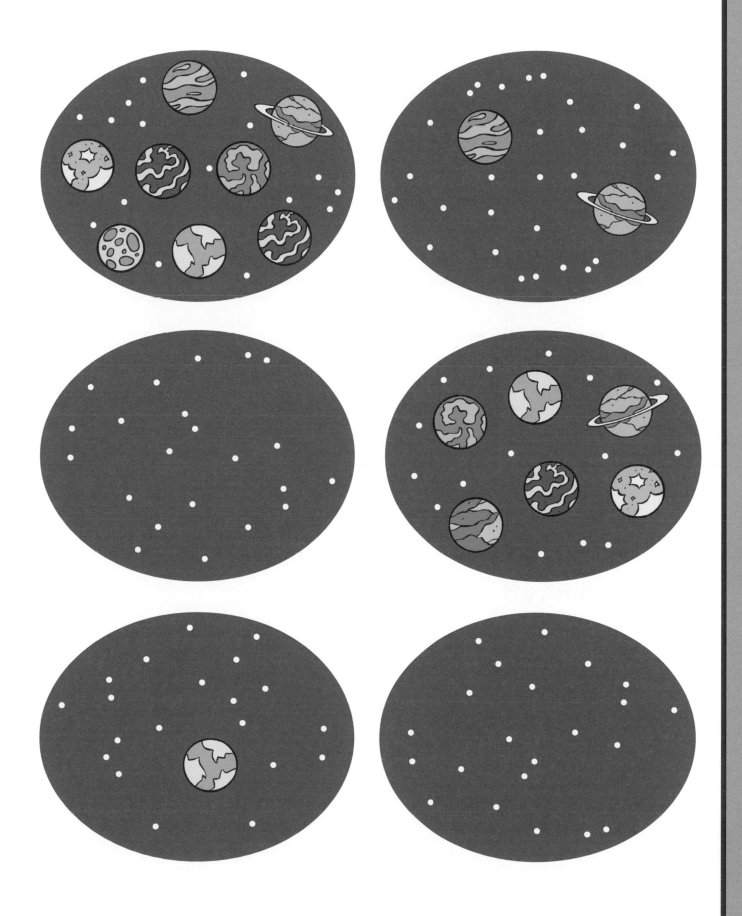

I one

Count the droid on the card.

Trace each I.

Start at the red dot.

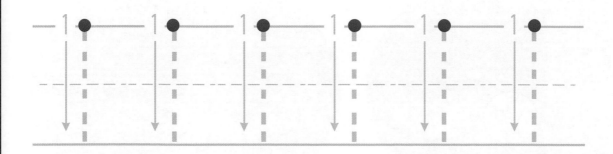

Touch and count each droid.

Circle everything that there is only **1** of in the picture.

2 two

Count the suns on the card.

Trace each **2**.

Start at the red dot.

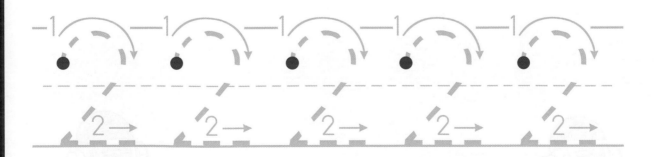

Touch and count the suns in each group.

Circle the groups of **2**.

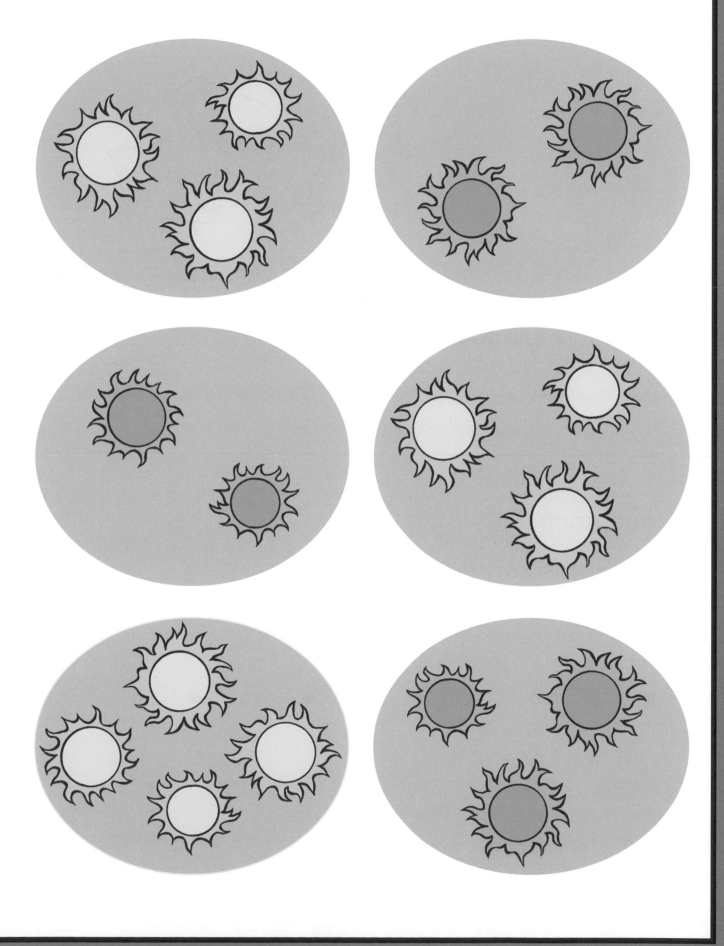

3 three

Count the tauntauns on the card.

Trace each **3**.

Start at the red dot.

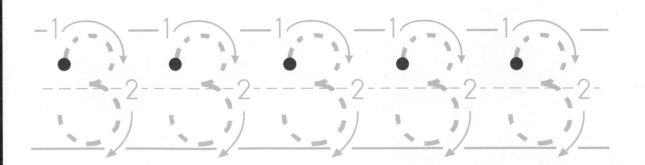

Touch and count the tauntauns in each group.

Circle the groups of **3**.

4 four

Count the starships on the card.

Trace each **4**.

Start at the red dot.

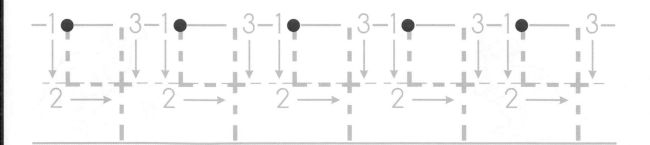

Touch and count the starships in each group.

Circle the groups of **4**.

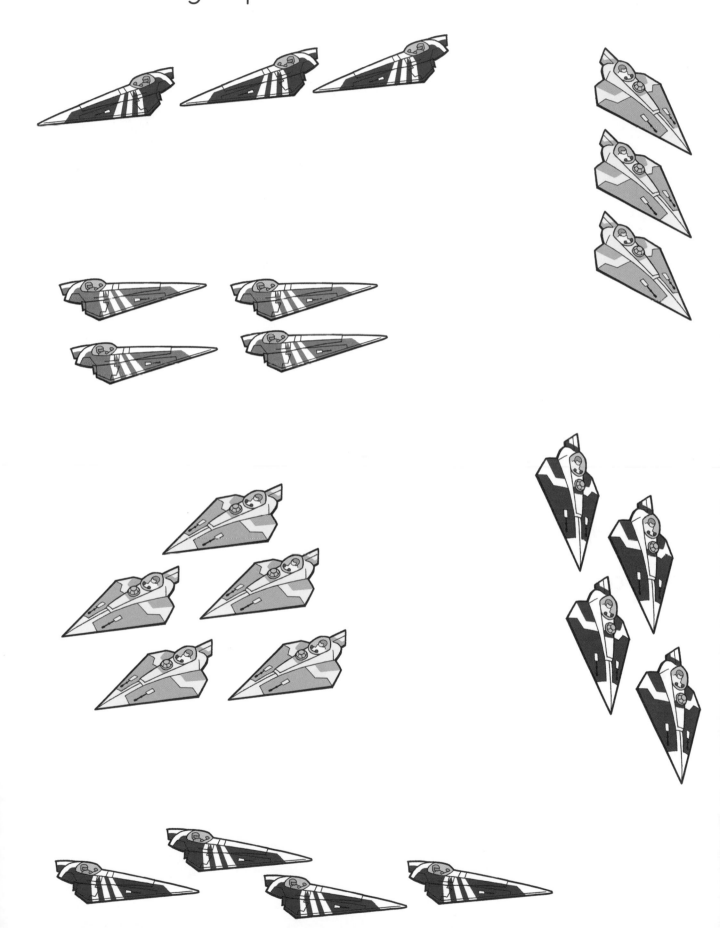

5 five

Count the Wookiees on the card.

Trace each **5**.

Start at the red dot.

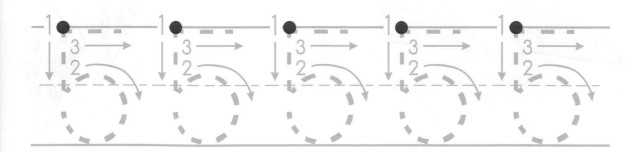

Touch and count the Wookiees in each group.

Circle the groups of **5**.

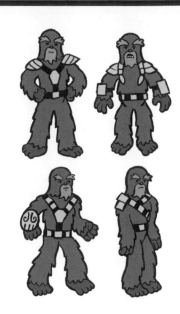

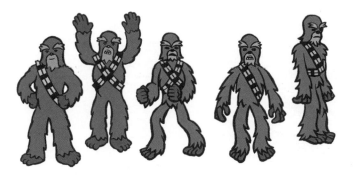

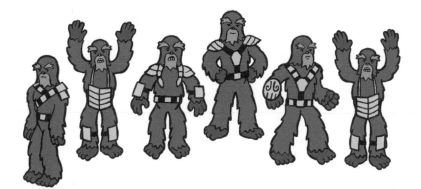

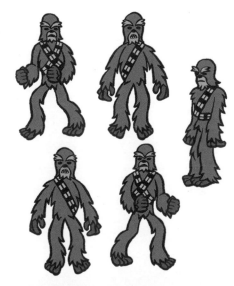

6 six

Count the lightsabers on the card.

Trace each 6.

Start at the red dot.

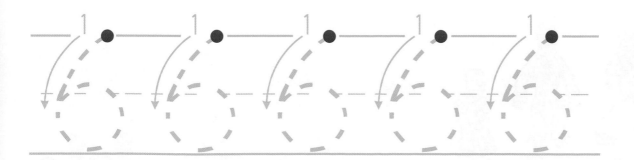

Touch and count the lightsabers in each group.

Circle the groups of 6.

7 seven

Count the Jawas on the card.

Trace each 7.

Start at the red dot.

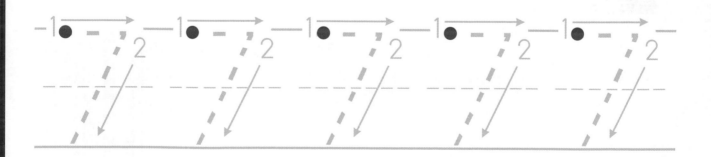

Touch and count the Jawas in each group.

Circle the groups of 7.

8 eight

Count the Ewoks on the card.

Trace each **8**.

Start at the red dot.

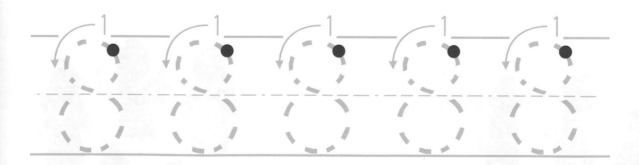

Touch and count the Ewoks in each group.

Circle the groups of **8**.

q nine

Count the clone troopers on the card.

Trace each 9.

Start at the red dot.

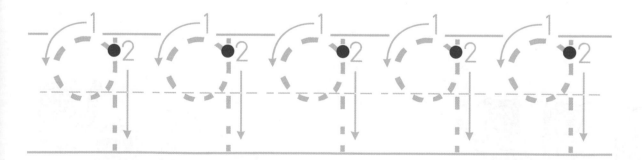

Touch and count the
clone troopers in each group.

Circle the groups of **9**.

10 ten

Count the Jedi on the card.

Trace each 10.

Start at the red dot.

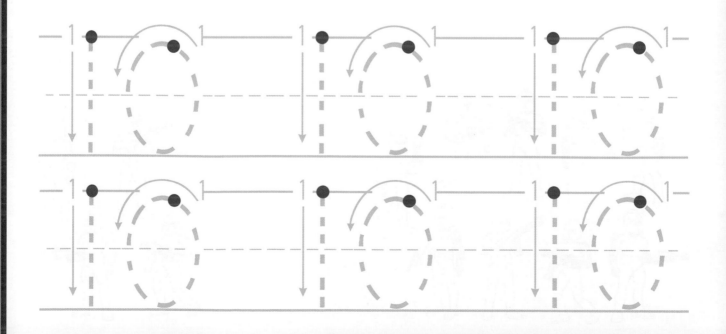

Touch and count the Jedi in each group.

Circle the groups of 10.

Colour 1 to 10!

Colour **1** mountain **purple**.

Colour **2** suns **yellow**.

Colour **3** lizards **green**.

Colour **4** droids **grey**.

Colour **5** Wookiees **brown**.

Colour **6** landspeeders **red**.

Colour **7** TIE Fighters **black**.

Colour **8** moons **blue**.

Colour **9** meteors **orange**.

Colour **10** flowers **pink**.

Cantina!

How many musical instruments of each kind do you see?

Draw a line from each group of instruments to the matching number.

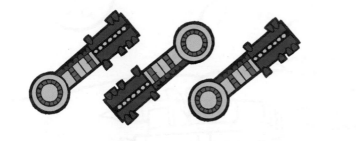

1

2

3

4

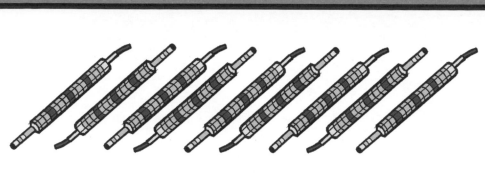

5

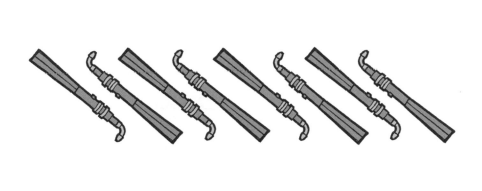

6

7

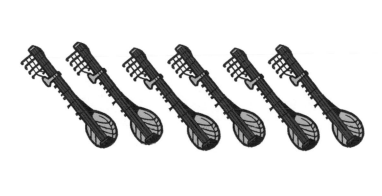

8

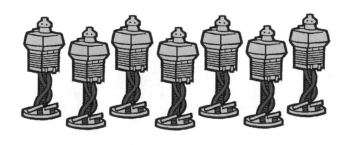

9

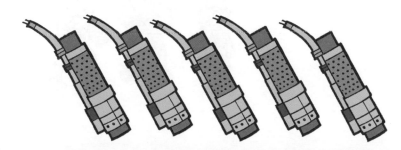

10

Count to 10!

Touch and count the characters and objects.

Trace the numbers.

 1

 2

3

4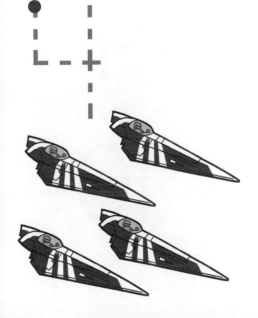

5

6

7

8

9

10

Buckle My Shoe!

Trace the missing numbers as you
sing "1, 2, Buckle My Shoe!"

1, 2, buckle my shoe.

3, 4, shut the door.

5, 6, pick up sticks.

7, 8, close the gate.

9, 10, let's count again!

Now trace all the numbers.

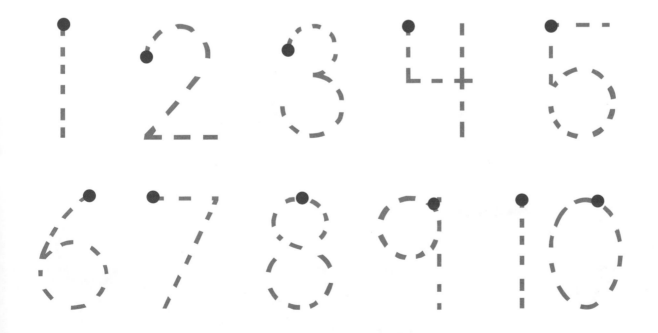

1 2 3 4 5
6 7 8 9 10

Ewok Dots!

Touch and count the dots on each Ewok.

Draw a line from each Ewok to the matching number.

Finger Match-up!

Count the fingers each hand or pair of hands is holding up.

Draw a line from the hand to the matching number.

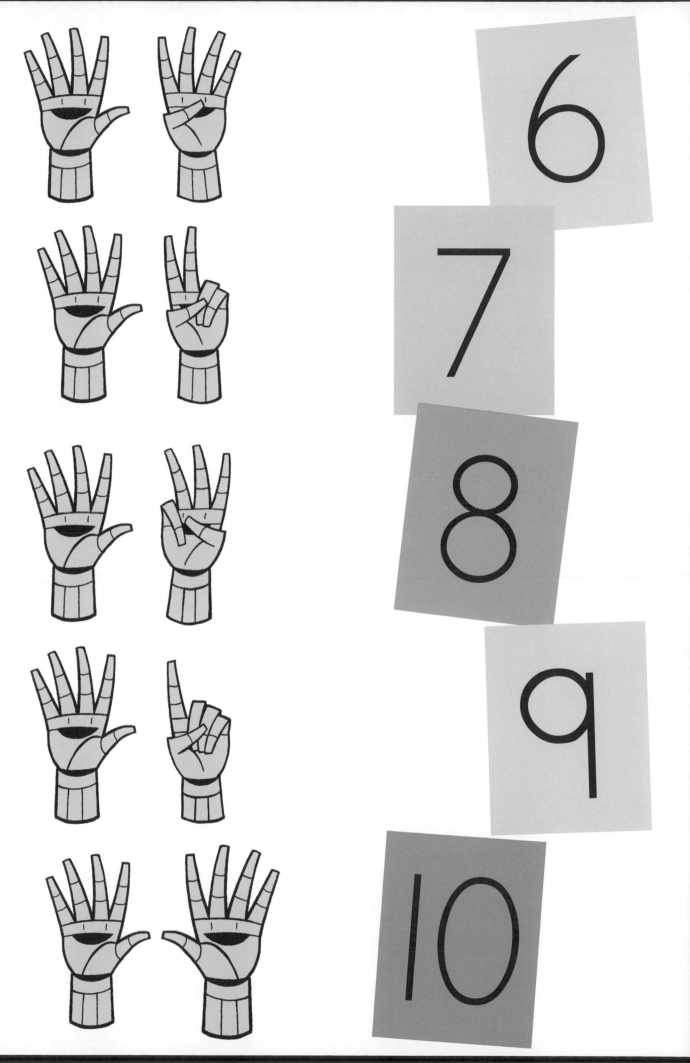

Tatooine!

Count the objects in each group on each card.

Circle the two groups on each card that have the **same** number.

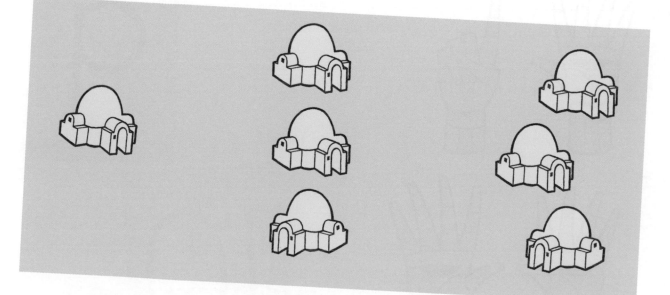

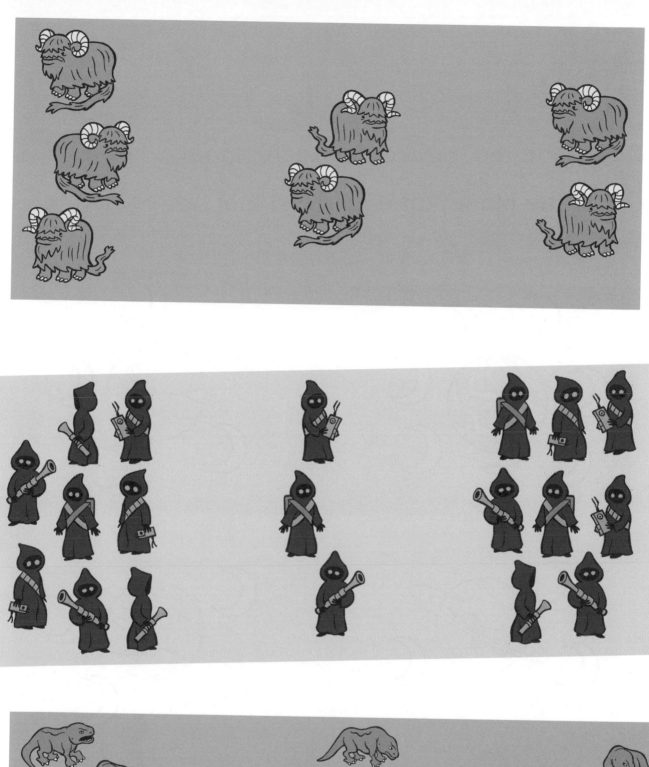

Moons!

Count the moons around each planet.

Circle the planet on each card that has **fewer** moons.

Coins!

Count the coins in each hand.

Circle the hand on each card with **more** coins.

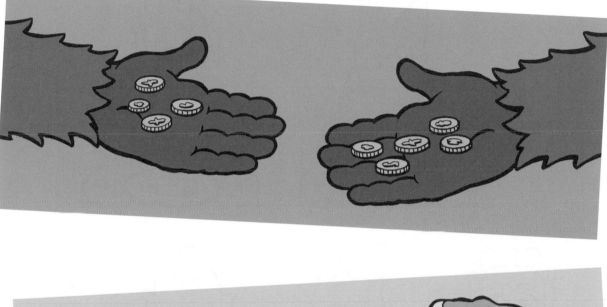

Cantina!

How many objects does each alien have?

Circle the alien on each card who has **most**.

Endor!

How many objects does each Ewok have?

Circle the Ewok on each card who has **fewer**.

Connect Dots!

Who is in the forest?

Connect the dots in number order from 1 to 10.

Connect Squares!

Who is in the starship?

Connect the squares in number order from 1 to 10.

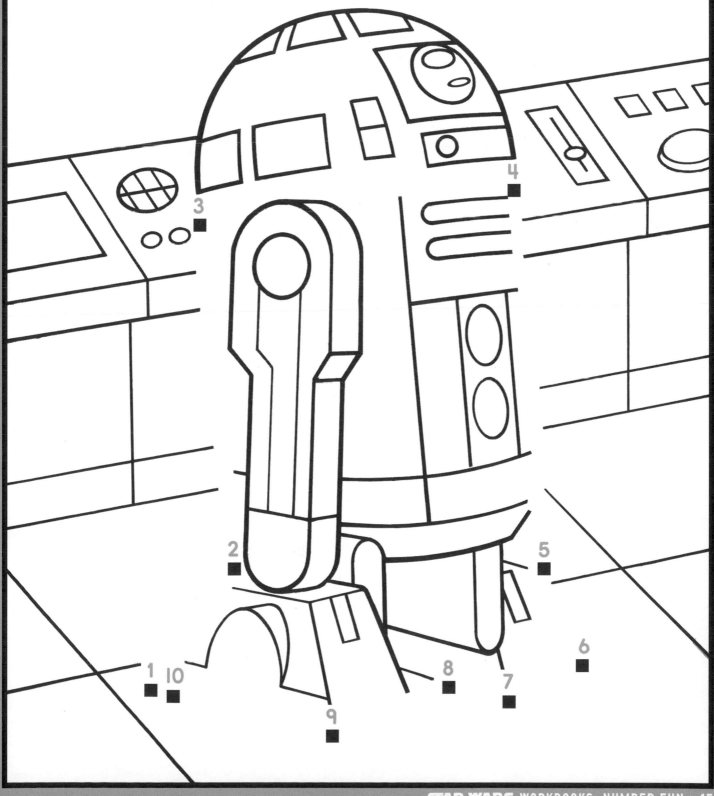

Count Down!

Trace the missing numbers as you help
R2-D2 count down to lift-off!

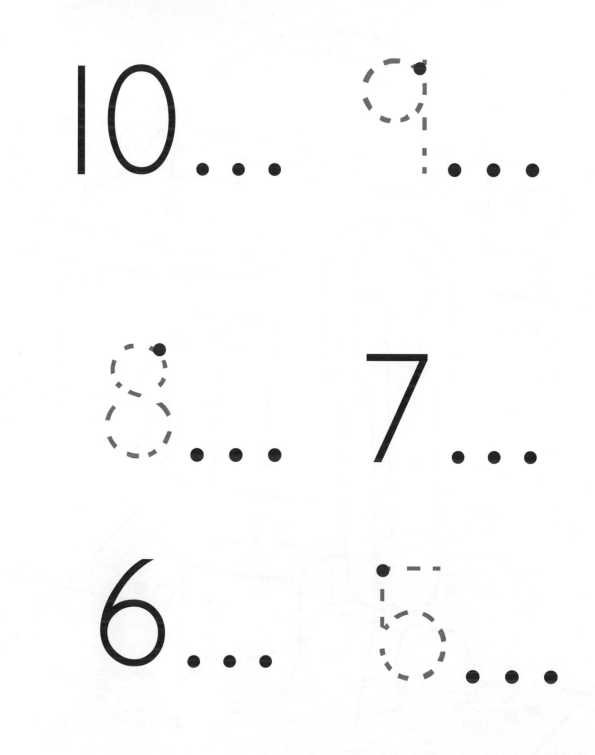

10...   9...

8...   7...

6...   5...

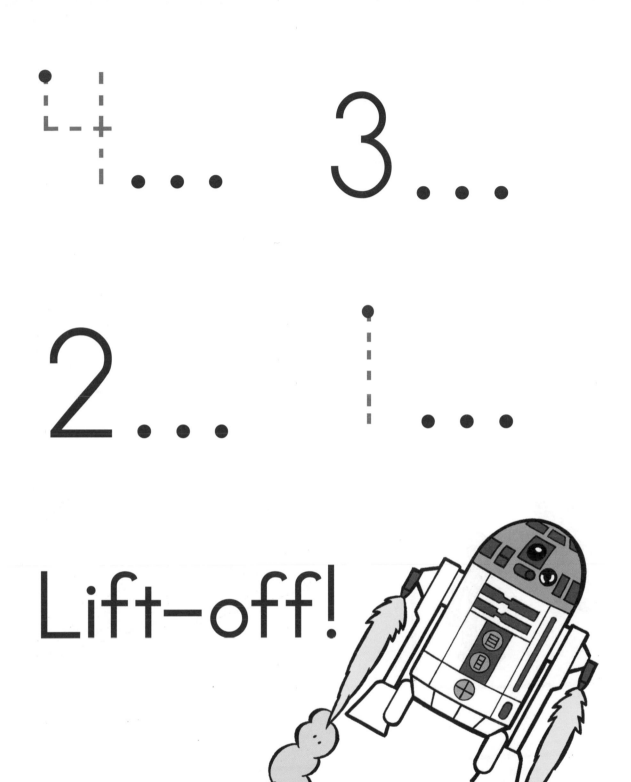

4... 3...

2... 1...

Lift-off!

Count and Colour!

Count the objects on each card.

Colour the card with **1**, **green**.

Colour the card with **2**, **orange**.

Colour the card with **3**, **yellow**.

Colour the card with **4**, **red**.

Colour the card with **5**, **blue**.

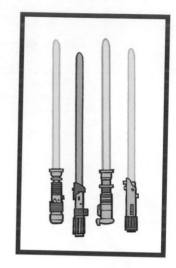

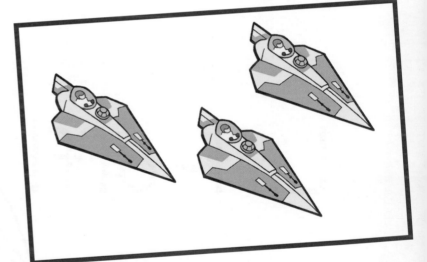

Count the objects on each card.

Colour the card with **6**, **blue**.

Colour the card with **7**, **red**.

Colour the card with **8**, **orange**.

Colour the card with **9**, **green**.

Colour the card with **10**, **yellow**.

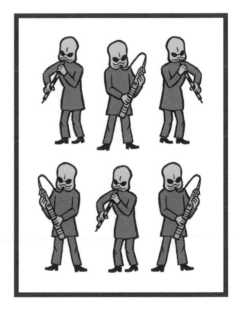

Write 0 to 5!

Trace each **0**.

Start at the red dot.

Trace each **1**.

Start at the red dot.

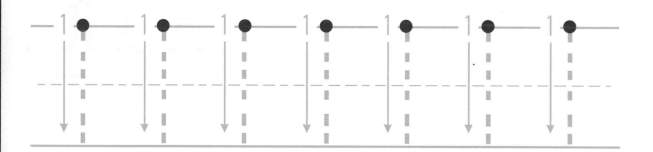

Trace each **2**.

Start at the red dot.

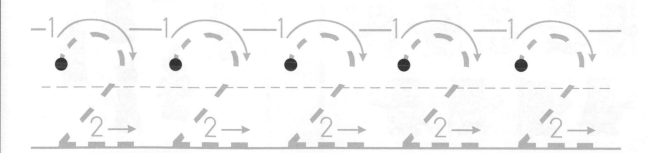

Trace each **3**.

Start at the red dot.

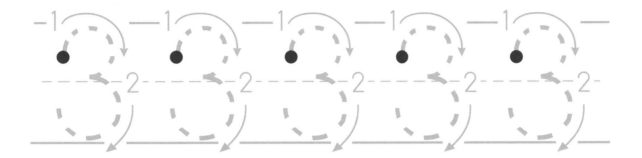

Trace each **4**.

Start at the red dot.

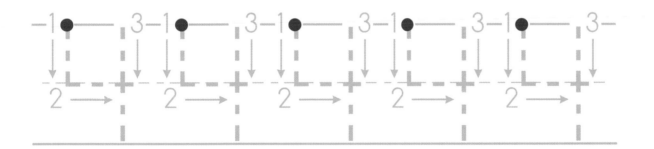

Trace each **5**.

Start at the red dot.

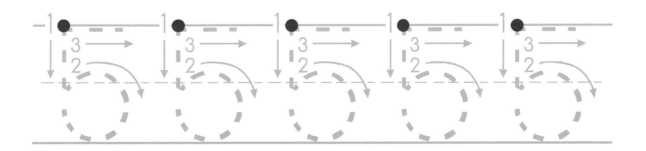

Write 6 to 10!

Trace each **6**.

Start at the red dot.

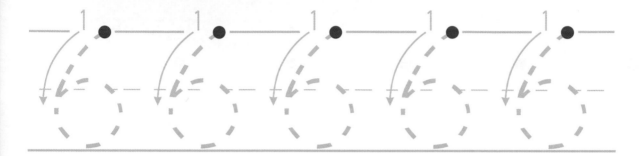

Trace each **7**.

Start at the red dot.

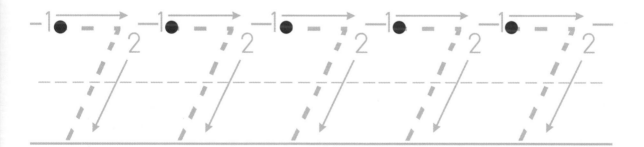

Trace each **8**.

Start at the red dot.

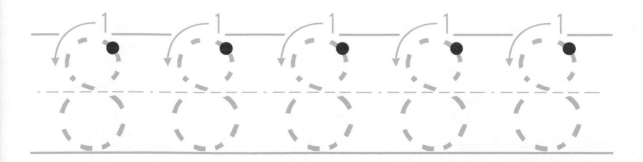

Trace each **9**.

Start at the red dot.

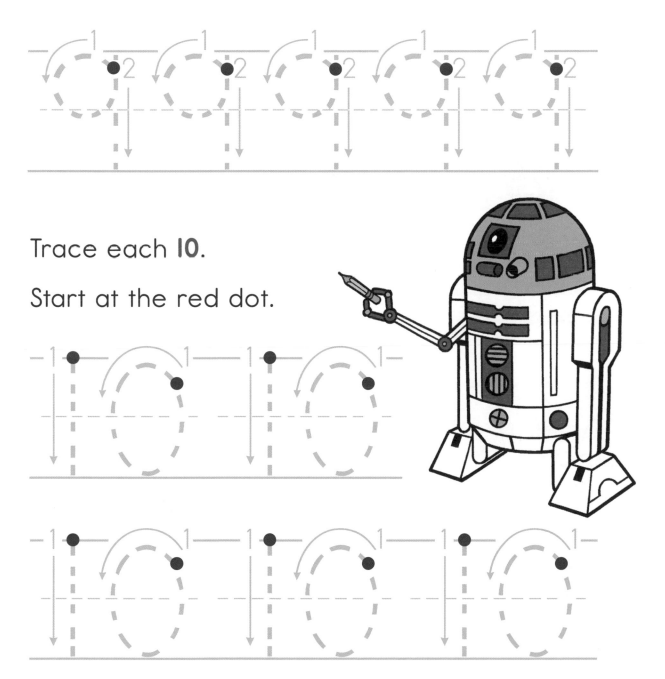

Trace each **10**.

Start at the red dot.

Naboo!

Count the objects in each group on each card.

Circle the two groups on each card that have the **same** number.

Count the Stars!

Touch and count the stars around each starship.

Draw a line from each group of stars to the matching number.

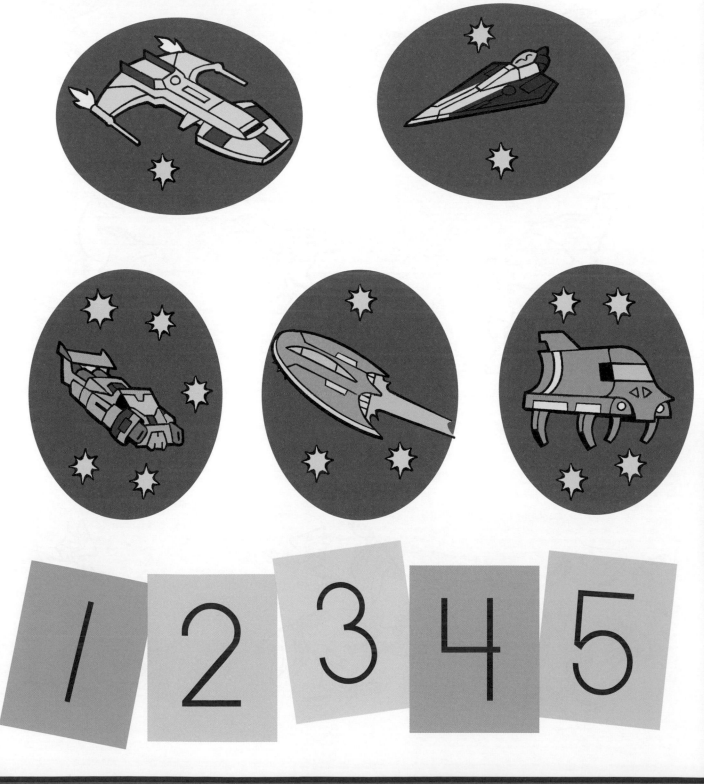

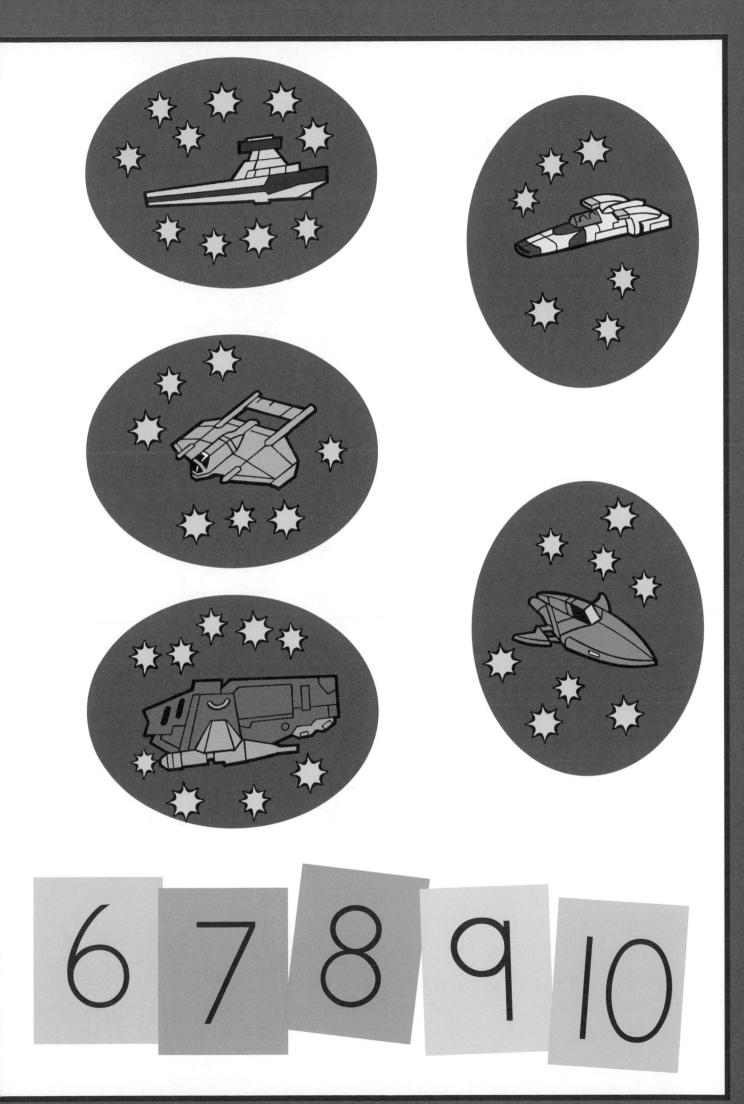

Write Numbers!

Trace the missing numbers next to each picture.

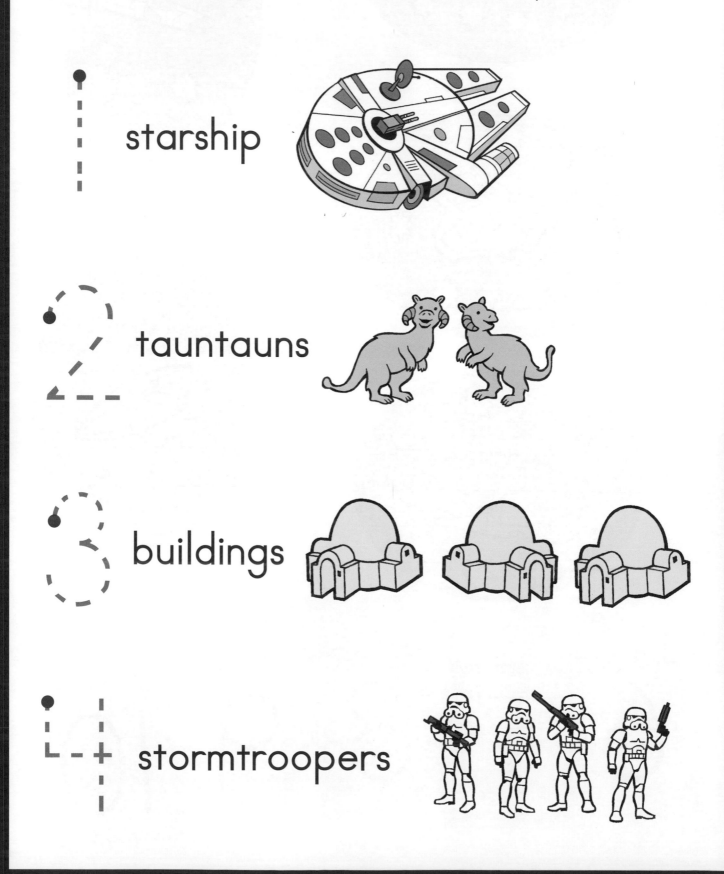

1 starship

2 tauntauns

3 buildings

4 stormtroopers

5 lightsabers

6 planets

7 Jawas

8 Twi'leks

9 stars

10 Ewoks

Trees!

Circle the trees that have **0** apples.

Starships!

Circle everything that there is only **I** of in the picture.

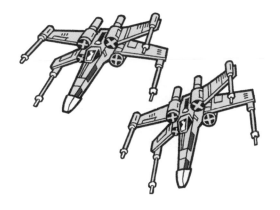

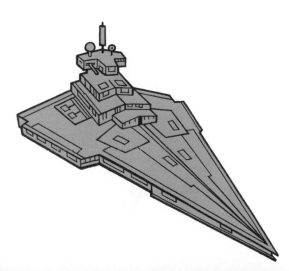

Lightsabers!

Circle the Jedi holding **2** lightsabers.

Rebel Alliance!

Circle the groups of **3**.

Creatures!

Circle the groups of 4.

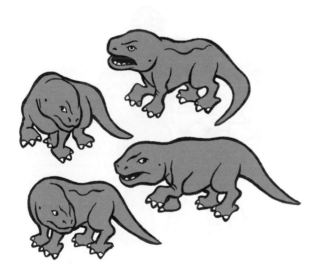

Buildings!

Circle the groups of **5**.

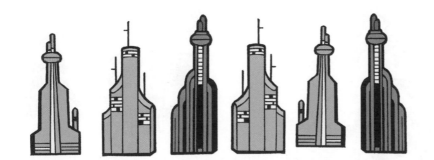

Battle Droids!

Circle the groups of **6**.

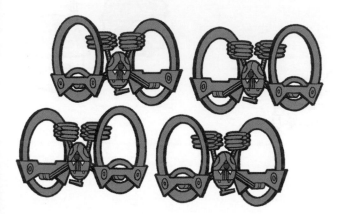

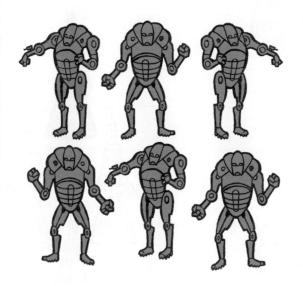

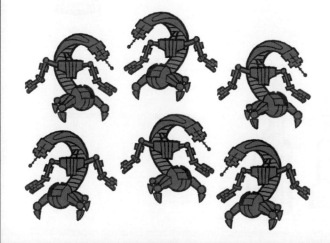

Species!

Circle the groups of **7**.

Scary Creatures!

Circle the groups of **8**.

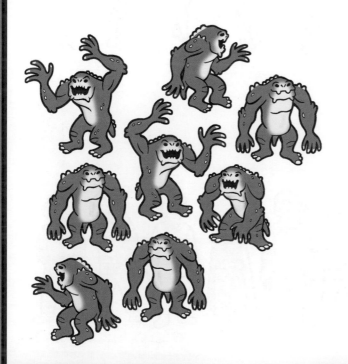

Troopers!

Circle the groups of 9.

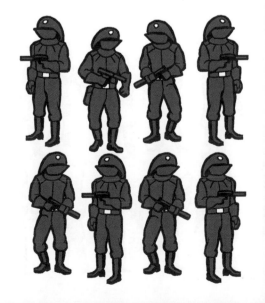

Cantina Players!

Circle the groups of 10.

Wookiees!

How many objects does each Wookiee have?

Circle the Wookiee on each card who has **more**.

Practise

Trace each **0**.

Start at the red dot.

Trace each **1**.

Start at the red dot.

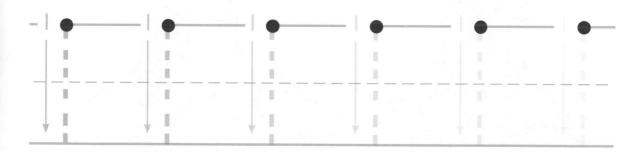

Trace each **2**.

Start at the red dot.

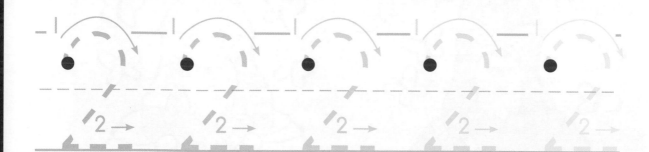

Trace each **3**.

Start at the red dot.

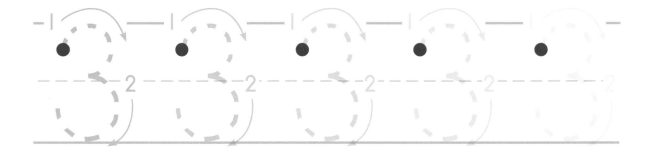

Trace each **4**.

Start at the red dot.

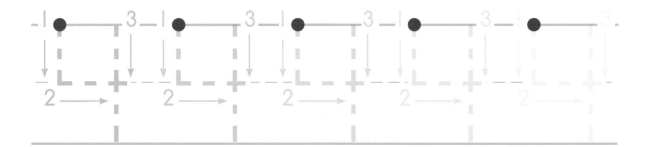

Trace each **5**.

Start at the red dot.

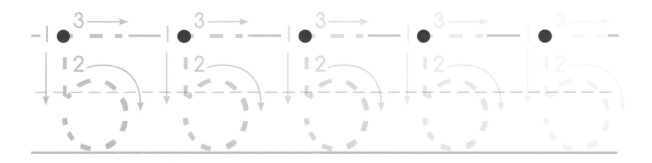

Practise

Trace each **6**.

Start at the red dot.

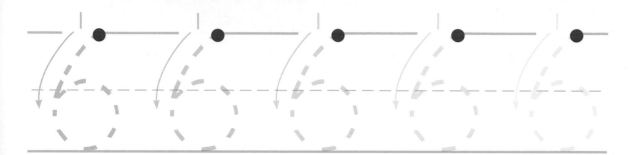

Trace each **7**.

Start at the red dot.

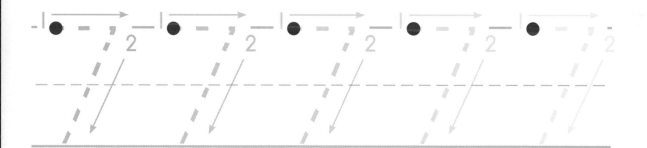

Trace each **8**.

Start at the red dot.

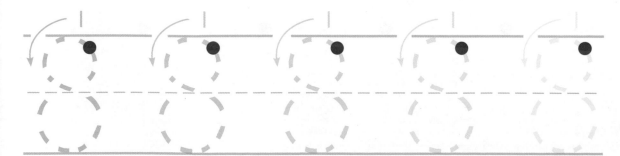

Trace each **9**.

Start at the red dot.

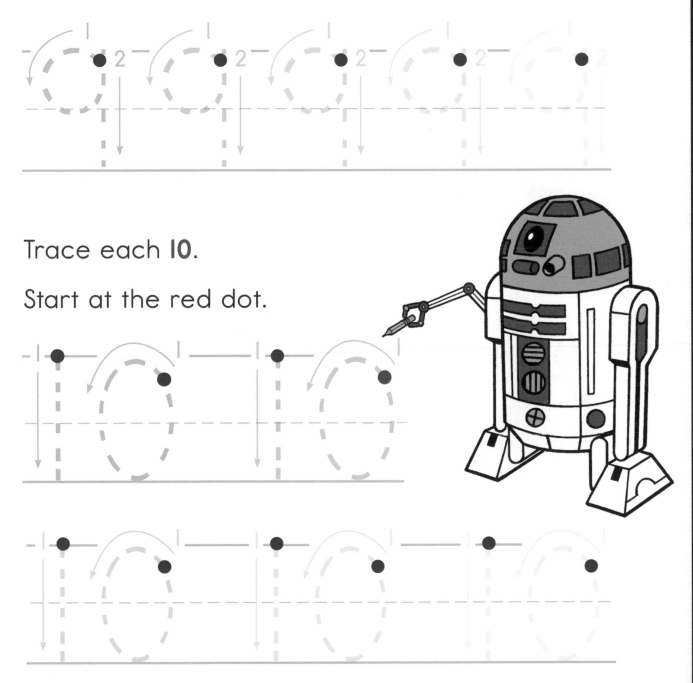

Trace each **10**.

Start at the red dot.

Landspeeders!

Touch and count the aliens in each landspeeder.

Draw a line from each landspeeder
to the matching number.

The Empire!

Count the objects in each group on each card.

Circle the two groups on each card that have the **same** number.

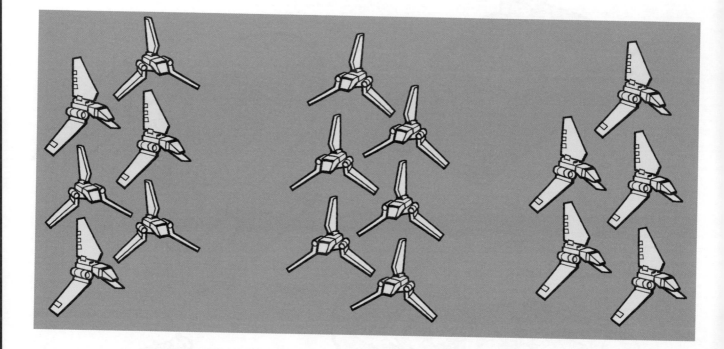

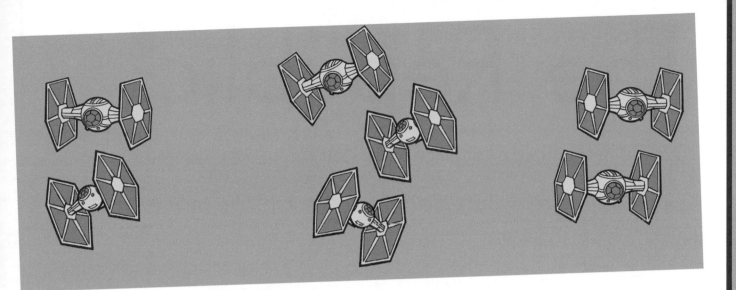

The Republic!

Count the objects on each card.

Circle the group on each card that has **more** objects.

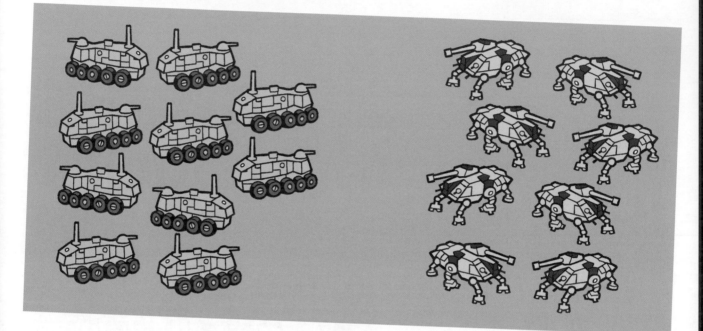

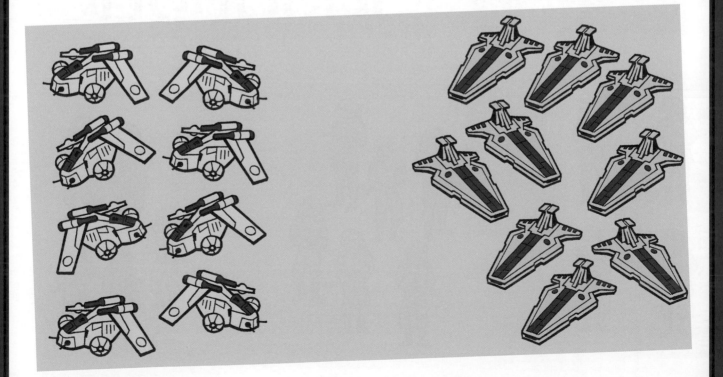

The Separatists!

Count the objects on each card.

Circle the group on each card that has **fewer** objects.

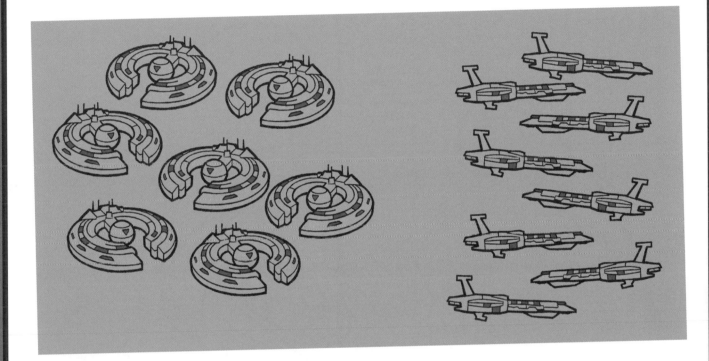

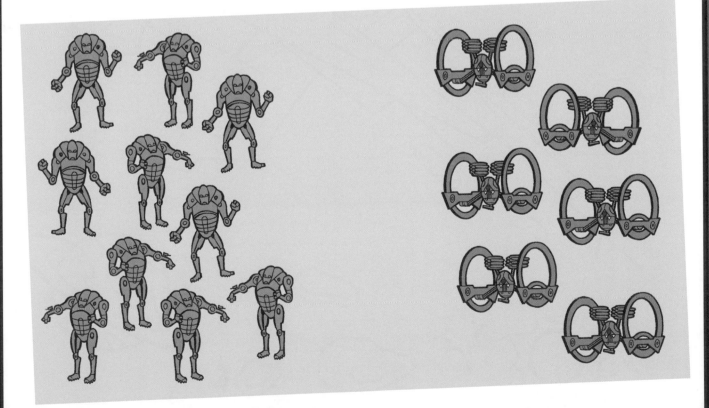

Connect Stars!

What is in outer space?

Connect the stars in number order from 1 to 10.

Connect Triangles!

Who is in the city?

Connect the triangles in number order from 1 to 10.

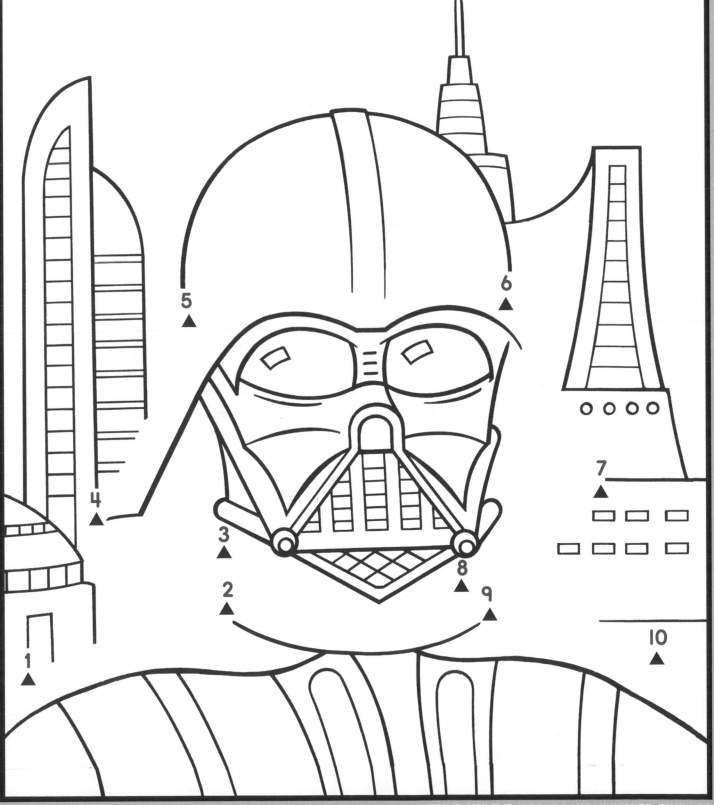

Next Number!

Trace the number that comes next.

0, 1

0, 1, 2

1, 2, 3

1, 2, 3, 4

1, 2, 3, 4, 5

5, 6

5, 6, 7

6, 7, 8

7, 8, 9

8, 9, 10

Same Number!

Trace the number on each card.

Circle the group that has the **same** number.

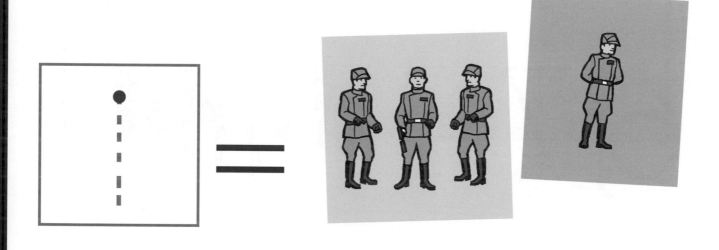

Same Number!

Trace the number on each card.

Circle the group that has the **same** number.

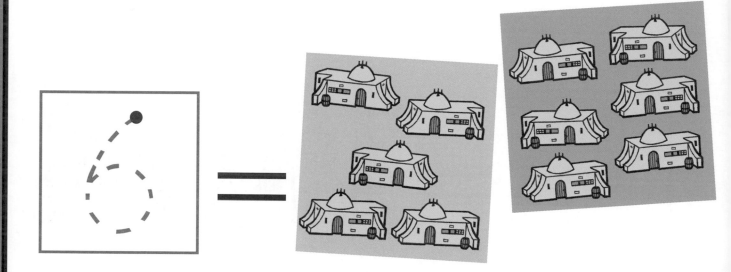

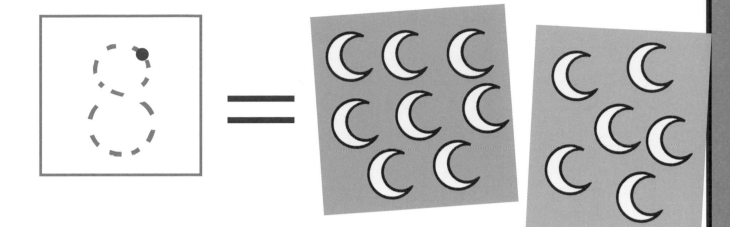

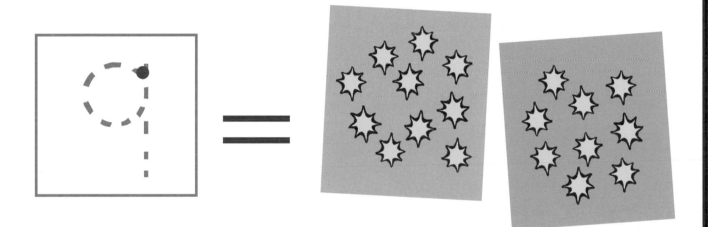

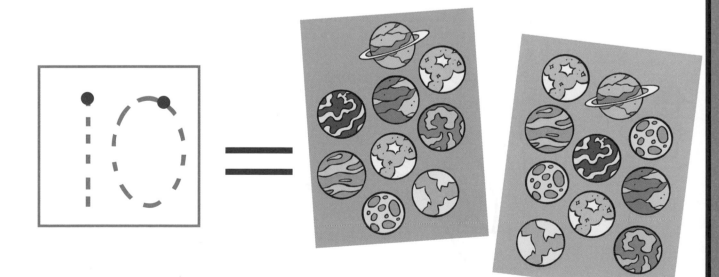

Now you can count from 1 to 10!

Are you ready to have more fun with *Star Wars*?

Make some finger puppets!

Using the templates on the following pages, ask an adult to follow the instructions to cut, fold and glue together finger puppet versions of *Star Wars* characters.

What you need:

- Finger puppet templates

- Safety scissors

- Sticky tape or glue

Finger Puppets

1 Ask an adult to cut out each finger puppet.

2 Curve the rectangular piece at the bottom of each puppet.

3 Ask an adult to tape or glue together the yellow marked areas.

4 Place finger puppets on your fingers!

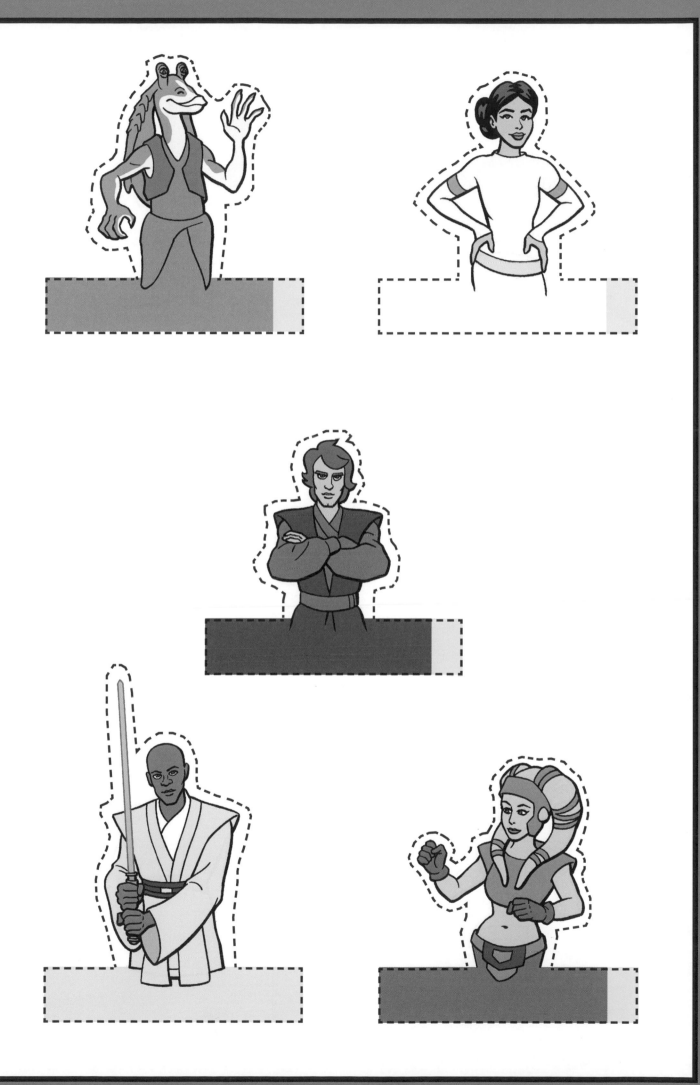

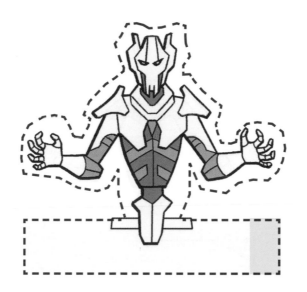

TN 16/3/18

Star Wars Workbooks: Number Fun
Scholastic Ltd
©LFL

Star Wars Workbooks: Number Fun
Scholastic Ltd
©LFL

Star Wars Workbooks: Number Fun
Scholastic Ltd
©LFL

Star Wars Workbooks: Number Fun
Scholastic Ltd
©LFL